I0459338

Written by: Patty Liu
llustrated by: Patty Liu
Edited by: Drew Tilton
Designed by: Amber Griffith

Library of Congress Control Number: 2024921063 | Hardcover ISBN: 979-8-9915015-0-7
Paperback: 979-8-9915015-1-4 | Ebook: 979-8-9915015-2-1

Copyright © 2025 by Patricia K Liu. All rights reserved. No part of this publication may be reproduced or transmitted in any manner or any form, whether electronic or mechanical, including photocopy, recording, or any storage and retrieval system that exists without the prior written permission of the copyright owner.

To request permission, contact the publisher at instalambkins.com.

First edition May 2025

Published by Patricia K Liu
instalambkins.com
@instalambkins

The Lambkin's Shepherd

Discovering the Way Home

Written and Illustrated by Patty Liu

Dedicated to:

The Shepherd

He personally invited me into
his flock where I have finally
found a family to belong to.

May you, too,
hear his voice, follow him,
and know his unwavering love,
as you grow in the desire
to become his lambkin.

Join me on this
adventurous journey
of discovery.

With joy,
Patty Liu

Lord, you are my *Shepherd*;

thank you so much. I have all I need!

It is so wonderful when you guide me to green pastures

and lead me to rest beside quiet pools of fresh water.

Baah, baah, BAAAAAAH!

Help, I am stuck...

Shepherd!

Thank goodness, *Shepherd*!
When I am upside down and stuck,
you come to upright me.

You renew my strength.

You show me the way as promised.

When I walk through
deep dark times
in the valley of death's shadow,

I will be brave.

Lord, I know you are with me.

Both your *Shepherd's* rod and staff
keep me safe and sound.

You prepare a deliciously scrumptious banquet feast for me,

where all my enemies can see me.

You bless and anoint my head with oil.

Shepherd, such love and protection
make me bubble over with joy in my heart.

You shower me with goodness and love.

Surely, you will be with me every day of my life.

And your house, the place
where we gather as the *Shepherd's* flock,
will be my home as long as I live.

Psalm 23

INV (InstaLambkins New Version)

Lord, you are my Shepherd;
thank you so much. I have all I need!

It is so wonderful when you guide me to green pastures
and lead me to rest beside quiet pools of fresh water.

Baah, baah, BAAAAAAH! Help, I am stuck... Shepherd!

Thank goodness, Shepherd!
When I am upside down and stuck,
you come to upright me.

You renew my strength.
You show me the way as promised.

When I walk through deep dark times
in the valley of death's shadow,
I will be brave.

Lord, I know you are with me.
Both your Shepherd's rod and staff keep me safe and sound.

You prepare a deliciously scrumptious banquet feast for me,
where all my enemies can see me.

You bless and anoint my head with oil.
Shepherd, such love and protection
make me bubble over with joy in my heart.

You shower me with goodness and love.
Surely, you will be with me every day of my life.
And your house, the place where we gather as
the Shepherd's flock, will be my home as long as I live.

Special Acknowledgements

After my parents' passing, I was invited to spend the weekend with my close friend Ellen and her mom, Beverlie. They welcomed me into their family and made me feel loved. Over a cup of tea in her home, Mama Bev asked me how my lambkin drawings came to be. I shared the comfort I had found in Psalm 23 while grieving the losses of my mom and dad, how God used the psalm to turn my mourning into joy. As we continued in conversation, this mother-daughter duo encouraged me to creatively bring this psalm to life using my lambkin drawings. This was the genesis of this book, and I am so thankful for these wonderful friends.

I am also grateful to Derek and Nancy's family, Steve and Diane, Drew, Chad, Amber, and Wendy Ida.

Since beginning the creation of this book, Mama Bev and Nancy are now in heaven with the Lord, my mom, and my dad. They are with Him, He is with them, and He is with me. In that way they are still with me today, in my heart also. If they were here in person, I would celebrate with them, saying, "The book is complete! Praise the Lord, the Shepherd!"

Finally, thank you, dear lambkins, for journeying with God and me. I pray you discover his deep, all-encompassing, genuine, and unconditional love.

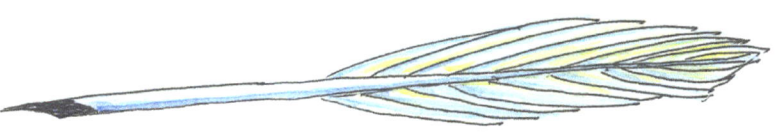

INK

Patty Liu loves to express herself and share her life with others through her doodles and illustrations. Sketchbook in hand, she begins each morning with a cup of tea and time with the *Shepherd*. She hopes that you, too, will find the hope and the joy and the love that she has found with him.

A portion of the proceeds from this book will go towards helping children in need in Patty's local community.

@instalambkins

www.ingramcontent.com/pod-product-compliance
Lightning Source LLC
Chambersburg PA
CBHW041618120626
46551CB00003B/494